The Vade Mecum of the True Sublime

liber hymnorum saecularium

omnia obstat

Poems by Bill Gillard

Imprimatur: R. Davies, VGPS

Luchador Press
Big Tuna, TX

Copyright © William Gillard, 2020
First Edition1 3 5 7 9 10 8 6 4 2
ISBN: 978-1-952411-12-0
LCCN: 2020937859

Cover image: Judith Baker Waller
Author photo: Imogen Gillard
All rights reserved. No part of this publication may be reproduced or transmitted in any form or by any means, electronic or mechanical, including photocopying, recording or by info retrieval system, without prior written permission from the author.

Acknowledgments:

Thank you to Jason at Luchador Press for believing in this collection. Thanks to Rob Stauffer for his sage advice and mad proofreading skillz. Thanks to Susan, Imogen, and Gwen for their love and support during the years it took me to write this book and especially for helping me to set up my work area in the basement during our shared quarantine in the spring of 2020.

"Autology," *Leaves of Ink,* Winter 2018, "Diamond Head," *Dark Sky Magazine,* November 2007, "Diorama," (formerly titled "Life on Earth") *Invisible Ink Poetry,* Winter 2009, "Divide," *Mountain Gazette,* October 2008, "Dragons in Subway Tunnels," *House of the Tomato,* 2015, "God the Father," *Meditations on Divine Names,* ed. Maja Trochimczyk, Moonrise Press, 2012, "Her Squid Uncooked," *House of the Tomato,* 2015, "If You Love Jesus, and If Heaven's Got a Barbed Wire Fence," *Meditations on Divine Names* ed. Maja Trochimczyk, Moonrise Press, 2012, "Ironbound," *House of the Tomato,* 2015, "Jeremy, the Boot Camp God," *SNReview 9.3,* Autumn 2007, "Low Tide, Passaic River, Lyndhurst, New Jersey," *Invisible Ink Poetry,* Winter 2009, "Love Stings Drone" and "Lonely," *Dime Show Review,* Fall 2017, "Moreno's Son," *Stickman Review 7.1,* Summer 2008, "Old Man, Drawn Brightly," *Gateways 1.1,* 2017, "Ranger Flight Roger, Point Pleasant," *New Jersey Review, Americana 2.2,* Fall 2007, "Rhinoceros," *Poetry Bay,* Fall 2006, "Sheol Farm," *Serving House: A Journal of Literary Arts,* Fall 2017, "Sometimes a Charcoal Drawing," *Gateways 1.1,* 2017, "Stafford's Deer," *Invisible Ink Poetry,* Winter 2009, "Strawberry Jam Apocalypse," *The Wisconsin Poets' Calendar,* 2008, "The Comet She Hoped Was a God," *Star Line,* Spring 2007, "The Secret of Electricity," *The Poetry Journal,* Spring 2008

Oremus

Especially for those unfamiliar with supplication to imaginary omnipotents, it is helpful to page through the entire collection first, stopping here and there to get a feel for how the prayer book unfolds. Practice good breathing habits during this phase.

Afterward, and as your devotion matures, it is existentially safest to read this book in its entirety every day, preferably aloud (clothing optional). Then nobody will be able to say that whatever comes next is your fault. You gave it your best shot. You were devout. Pious, even.

The sequence of the day is as follows:

matins to be read during all-night philosophy wind-ups with lovers and ex-lovers; use soft tones; invent a new kind of afterlife to scare each other; read these when both of you are propped up on elbows and pillows, the window cracked open to feed to the night what you've left unspoken between you

lauds read these at dawn when you're not yet guilty of anything in particular but you have a strong feeling that this day will bring you something woeful because they all do

hora media read these at midday, the time to reflect on the few opportunities that remain as the light dwindles; these are especially urgent for winter when the day is about six hours shorter than it is during the summer; remember to floss

vespers these are your evening prayers, to be recited as the sun sets; at some point, you need to give up; tomorrow is another day to locate what it is inside you that you were sure you had when you were sixteen; those better than you are waves pounding on the beach; at vespers, you are the beach, fragmented, trod upon

compline bed yourself alone or not—it does not matter—when you've run out of good options; these aloud can postpone your despair, which is the sole power of prayer, by filling the air with the warmth from your mouth; the average ambient temperature of the universe is negative 454° F; express these like prayers for minus 450° and you might keep the braying Kierkegaard outside your window for another night

Novices may use their own local time. Acolytes may choose to use North American Eastern Standard and Daylight Time to better synchronize their prayers with those of the man you just stepped over on the subway grate at the corner of 14th Street and 8th Avenue.

Adiunctum, which occur on feast days (mother's date of birth or death, the anniversary of a traumatic break-up that was clearly not your fault, e.g.), are noted in the relevant text.

PSALTER INRITUS

matins

Sheol Farm / 1

You Should Have Bought That Charcoal Drawing / 3

The Glint of Steel You'll Bite / 4

And She Photon Love's Mirrors Twin / 6

Where Miner Street Crosses the Grass / 8

Proof of the Existence of God / 11

Trinities / 13

Candy's House / 14

Ad Hostler Prayer / 19

A Glow in the East / 20

The Pale King / 22

Meditation: The Promotion of Juan Sebastián Elcano, New Master of the Victoria, the Spanish Carrack that Circumnavigated the Globe / 24

lauds

Sparse Talent Squandered / 29

Autogenes in the Fields / 31

Divide / 32

The 6 Train and the Omega / 33

The Rumor of Love / 35

Harm Lay I / 36

The Ancestor Story / 37

What Will Kill Him and Soon / 38

Old Man, Drawn Brightly / 39

RESPONSORIAL PSALM:

    The Comet She Hoped Was a God / 41

Crawled She New Booming Bed / 42

How to Pray to a Spider / 43

Private Property / 44

Meditation: Be Joyful! / 45

hora media

This Noncommittal Gravity / 49

A Martyr Made When Lustful Suitors Came / 51

Made Down Here by the Breaking of Things / 53

Ranger Flight Roger, Point Pleasant, New Jersey / 54

Reasons to be Cheerful, Part 4 / 56

On Our Reptilian Origin / 58

Any Precious, Fragile Thing / 59

Watergate / 60

You Ever Music Me / 61

Meditation: Healing of the Water / 63

vespers

Breakwater Serenade / 67

We Live Here / 69

The River in the Rain / 71

Moreno's Son / 72

Jeremy, the Boot Camp God / 73

Ironbound / 74

Dragons in Subway Tunnels / 75

Her Squid Uncooked / 77

A Theory of the Afterlife / 79

The Bad Knish / 81

All of the Optimistic Religions / 82

Meditation: What Do All the People Know? / 84

compline

Love Stings Drone and Lonely / 89

I Never Beat Her at Scrabble, Not Once / 91

Achingly Paisley-Less / 92

Stafford's Deer / 94

Strawberry Jam Apocalypse / 95

The Sound of Rain in a Bucket / 97

Not Pure Enough to Burn / 99

The Secret Of Electricity / 100

The Biologist and His Daughter / 103

All these things will be specified in time,
    With strict regard to Aristotle's rules,
The Vade Mecum of the true sublime,
    Which makes so many poets, and some fools:
Prose poets like blank-verse, I 'm fond of rhyme,
    Good workmen never quarrel with their tools;
I 've got new mythological machinery,
And very handsome supernatural scenery.

-Don Juan, Lord Byron

matins

The deep night, with the sun directly below your feet...

Sheol Farm

I awoke naked and cold and found myself at the edge of a dark
forest Jesus stood next to me he pointed into the black
wood and said come on Joe come on but I was tired and sore

from the things I'd done and I didn't feel much like taking a
walk so I pointed at the distant golden lights right there across
that field so close you could read the Bible by it I joked and
    Jesus spake

whatever the short cut home took us into a wide spinach
field heavy with cultivation Jesus wasn't happy he kind
of grumbled under his breath halfway across a dog

barked and the door of the farmhouse swung open
and flooded the green carpet with soft light we dropped
to the burying earth and looked out just above the dark

leaves a farmer stood outlined in his kitchen's yellow
who that out there he shouted you better run now go git'em
girl and we did run stumbling and crashing the dog's bark

and snarl closer and closer I laughed when Jesus tripped and
said his own name I asked him if it was a sin but he was out
of breath from running and said go to hell and kind of half

smiled so I figured we were golden but then he stopped
and didn't say a word let me run a few more steps right
into the fence how could he let me end up draped

over the field's barbed wire edge this close to home free
like laundry on a line every movement a fresh star of pain
like being stabbed by a stranger who wants your TV I told

you not to come this way he said and threw his robe over the
barbed wire next to me clambered up and over eyed me from
the other side get me down I cried but he just shook his head

sadly ankle deep in the soybeans of paradise and me hanging
up there food for crows and I couldn't help myself I laughed
and coughed this is me and it always has been yes Jesus said

yes tears rolled down my cheeks each coughing spasm drove
the thin rusted barbs like a serrated knife somebody might
find handy in a kitchen when the old man comes downstairs

a crash and a hiss and three dogs bit at my ankles and Jesus
was gone a gruff voice from the shadows you're mine now
the farmer said twin shotguns like wings on his shoulders

You Should Have Bought That Charcoal Drawing

from the back road antique store
a dark scene a monastery
a single man among many indistinct others
his eyes upraised
with one foot on the bottom step
of an ancient stairway
that twists upward through the roof
through the clouds into forever
you dream now about that picture
you can't get it out of your mind
had you the real thing
you'd study it to find out at last if you are the one
with one foot heavenward
or among the washed-out horde
for whom the stairway is an
incense-scented Sunday rumor
or worse

The Glint of Steel You'll Bite

bait me like the hook you drop
into the briny drink
troll me through the kelp and snag
my edges fraying rotten
you pride me like some shiny clasp
against East Village merit
to angle leather beamish boys
who hungry come to me
and I disposable your glitter
ingested then forgotten
at one with salted intestines
dissolved into another
this marriage of what once was me
and all you have discarded
to another being not like me
to serve your better nature
it's me they want but get the hook
(it's you I want… alas!)
I'll die digested fish is grilled
and you, you seem quite sated
part of me floats free in tides
and blends with grainy silt
freezes fast in skin of ice
evaporates to sky
and breathing deep you dine content
this oyster sewer world
that once grew fat and filtered me

on reefy reservation
so parts of me are now in you
ironic we should meet
in this café where we once prayed
and whispered teary hopes
but I'm no bait and you've no hook
ten blocks from the East River
I want to know before we dance
what metaphor will free me
how to conceive in lover's womb
the glint of steel you'll bite
I'm humming backbeat triplets flex
you're landing hard on quarters
I'm driving free on Utah salt
you train electric Sweden
I'm dancing to the big horn sound
you lecture in Hyannis
I am a cloud in starry sky
you're Doctor Jekyll's doctor
I'm free like ship chains wound on spools
you're wind and glass and pixies
If Springsteen covered Polyrock
I'm b-side instrumental
If Jesus covered JS Bach
you'd still live in my headphones

And She Photon Love's Mirrors Twin

a friend has married eight times now
I haven't met the latest
I'm sure she's young and indiscreet
I'm sure she's pink and gracious
flowing hair black like one before
and narrow hips and smile
a paperback in jeans back pocket
a pulp with ET form
she likes the classic sf best
not NG TOS
he picked her when they played Halo
she held her own when pressed
he picked her when she rattled off
her top ten Bauhaus songs
I see her now in my mind's eye
just like his first the one
we shared Rowena for a while
true she was my first too
and she photon love's mirrors twin
bounced lightspeed each between us
I didn't know what color was
until she luminized me
didn't know the world could shine
until she made it luster
and bounced off me her masslessness
knocked me back like thunder
a reaching arm at sublight speed

already interacted
my friend in joy and laughing loud
illuminated happy
I could not stop I called her back
and then he saw us kissing
it's science man and nothing more
special relativity
a friend has married eight times now
I haven't met her but
there's some for him and some for me
that still calls out Rowena!

Where Miner Street Crosses the Grass

she throws my keys off
the narrow steel bridge into
the shallow Grass River that
splashes under May's sharp moonlight

we descend the embankment toe
into the spring-thaw waters to
kick gravel for the keys
our way back to campus

she laughs and dares me
to object to stomp back
the Miner Street mile to
campus in the misty midnight

she touches my forearm and
presses her cold cheek to
mine saying now you can't
leave not now not ever

she dares me legs splayed
across a smooth boulder to
make something of her the
dark corners of her lips

pulled like a fitted sheet
over her teeth never quite
all the way to a
smile this woman I had

known in passing since September
who met me after work
tonight as if by coincidence
who bartered a pizza roll

for a night drive to
see the world because she
had no car the black
trees silhouetted against the black

North Country sky all life
in this northern town gone
black abed and here I
am begging May's brief night

to make me glib and
sexy my native tongue lacks
the syntax for one such
as she the May sky

pinks in the east I
think that's what Montreal would
look like under nukes it
isn't something I say out

loud I think please not
the dawn not dawn she
smiles at me through wet
bangs I think oh let

it be nuclear war and
not the dawn I'm not
ready yet for the dawn
it's only Montreal a small

price to pay for the
answer to her and me
soaked in fallout's first light
groping at fusion   but

then a car passes and
then four the day buzzes
to life above us on
that narrow steel bridge and

she tells me she splashed
a stone and not my keys
she had them all along
presses them into my palm

the talisman revealed we become
ourselves again to crawl from
this muck to walk as
sunlit strangers to my car

the silent ride to campus
to the lot where we
park what might have been
slink soaked away and fissioned

Proof of the Existence of God

at the Jesuit retreat house
up the Hudson with two
misters and two fathers and
fifteen friends the cool spring
day passed in a pollen-
dappled haze they asked us
questions about everything and all
doubts led us outside after
lights out first to the market
in town where we bought the
incongruous coconut held it high
for the passing cars one
        passing car
        brake lights
        u-turn
        high school angels answering prayers
        from open car windows
        brake lights like heaven's beams
        u-turn like redemption
        shirts lifted the heavens filled with stars
        a thrill for teenage believers
        the car sped off
        wait come back jesus come back
        no brake lights
        no u-turn
later on the night that
could not end me alone

walking down always downhill to
that great river's black track
under the train trestle lay
me down inches below the
rails to watch the stars
I must have dozed I
didn't hear the train coming
until it roared above me
sparks screaming the screech of
steel on steel startling me
sideways one leg one arm
over the edge hanging in
the air over the black
water the white chunks of
ice flowing by like bright
clouds passing above me and
below ice and clouds me
floating
downstream
melting
silent
majesty

Trinities

Bless you, Father,
for you need
it and no
confession can forgive
you for not
knowing the difference
between a hope
fervently desired and
the void. You
scream certainty at
the inchoate roar
you raise the
fist of religion
on a deck
akimbo when a
boy in your
care says he's
slipping down, down
storm-battered, arms
raised (you'd say
in prayer) into
the white cold,
dogma's hurricane breakers.

Candy's House

1.
a blue black bear shakes off the wet cold
nose alert
locks me eye to eye
chases me down the muddy road
panting and grunting at my back
up ahead on higher ground
a house just being built
roof on, but no windows yet
no interior finish
just roughed out
a place to hide
the bear is coming the bear
but inside
quiet
a closet
under the thin door's crack
the bear snuffles the dirt
the bear for whom scent is truth
shuffles away
silence

2.
I crack open the door
and look around
but the house has changed
years have passed

polished floors
track lighting on the ceiling
through the door into the kitchen
wide plank floors
stainless everything
and then my old friend
she enters says hello
like nothing ever happened and
she never died
she is as I remember her
smile under wispy too-long bangs
a tee shirt loose
tumbling off her shoulders
framing her face

3.
I remember Hawaii she says
and I do too
we were on the first plane
to land after the cyclone hit
Oahu was an island of wrecked flowers
the early summer blossoms
a petal storm
she said then and now
everywhere flowers
in the terminal
in tire treads
everywhere flowers and
Candy
everywhere

beauty and
destruction
the sweet smell of death and
life in her hair
for weeks
life and death

4.
then her son enters the kitchen
sits and smiles
shy
he looks nothing like me
she strokes his hair
pictures of his heroes on the wall and
a life taped to the refrigerator
he's a fine boy
through the window now roughed out
there's rustling in the underbrush
a bear I shout
but Candy smiles
a bear you say look again
and it's a shaggy dog
with bangs too long
it nuzzles the bottom step
trundles up the unpainted steps to
find love at Candy's feet
I know the way now
down the stairs into the day
one last time

5.
she shakes some world from
a gold leaf paper
it catches light
sparkles for a second
drops to me to the dirt below her tower
and on the gold these black letters
>	we are each of us in motion
>	the past is not fixed
>	chase dreams that scatter
>	like petals after a storm

I wanted to be beautiful for her
after all this time to
reveal myself in complexity
bitter majestic angry irresistible
predator and prey
bear and dog
I wanted to be
blood letters on gold paper
I wanted all of this
for her

6.
evening leaves turned the breeze
to a hissed good night
in my hand the gold
paper turned to brown leaf
and crumbled
the house devolved
into shadow

incomplete
unbuilt
windowless
a memory
empty
we are fallen leaves of autumns past

7.
at my back I hear the same low growl
I'd been running from
all these many years
but I know the way now
I remember the
thing she never forgot
not even for a minute
I know the way now
the thing she never forgot
she has been here all this time
I know the way now
I run toward
something
again
she has been here all this time
hoping to remind me
and I know the way now
toward
the thing she never forgot
something
I know
again

Ad Hostler Prayer

~~Our~~ Father, ~~who art in heaven,~~
~~hallowed be thy name,~~
thy kingdom ~~come,~~
~~thy~~ will be done,
on earth ~~as it is in heaven.~~
~~Give us~~ this day ~~our daily bread.~~
~~And forgive~~ ~~us~~ our trespasses,
~~as we forgive those who trespass against us.~~
~~And~~ lead us *not* into ~~temptation,~~
~~but deliver us from~~ evil.
~~For thine is the kingdom,~~
~~and the~~ power, and ~~the~~ glory,
forever. ~~Amen.~~

Father
thy kingdom
will be done
on earth this day

our trespasses
lead us into
evil, power,
and glory
forever

These are the words you are saying when you speak this prayer. The actual words. Remember that. Next time, stay silent except for these words. How does that feel? And did eternity respond this time?

A Glow in the East

I am a teacher
I should have known
the kid left so quickly each day
I could have stopped him
I promised that he'd have the
best weekend of his life
I made that promise to him on a Friday
I don't know why I said it
I never said anything like that before

        by Sunday night he was dead

instead I should have said this weekend
would be like many others dark mostly
with a glow in the east to raise our hopes

I wonder how he was found
by whom
when
a little sister
a mom
a father
and if I a guy who's known him for five weeks
rue the missed chances
how does a dad live
knowing that in those 19 years he had
7000 mornings and
how many chances

and this day
and the next
and the next
and the next
brings that glow in the east
to raise our hopes
that this sleepless night
will end in a day different
from the one before
or the one before that
or the endless horizon of tomorrows
without him

The Pale King

I have no great love for
his writing—it makes me
think about the words
and the mind that formed
those sounds that pound the
shore like waves at Chesil
whose stones are worn smooth
by the rushing in and out
petals in their
daily doing and
undoing on a black bough
where John Muir in his
spruce traveled miles by
treetop in a storm
words duned high and
porous the Kill Devil Hills
shift beneath
my feet whose summit
at Jockey's Ridge reveals
miles and miles of more
of the same brown and blue
horizon at an indifferent
distance

But dead?

How, dead?

From a rafter they said the sun-
dappled California afternoon
hillside that garage full of
words like old clothes for
the curb a few years shy of
vintage I sprawl and stare at the
story trying to pin the wriggling
metaphor to the wall that will
satisfy this reader at the end of
so many—and so few—pages

-for DFW

Meditation: The Promotion of Juan Sebastián Elcano, New Master of the Victoria, the Spanish Carrack that Circumnavigated the Globe

When our muskets were discharged, the natives would never stand still, but leaped hither and thither, covering themselves with their shields. They shot so many arrows at us and hurled so many bamboo spears (some of them tipped with iron) at the captain-general, besides pointed stakes hardened with fire, stones, and mud, that we could scarcely defend ourselves.

Seeing that, the captain-general sent some men to burn their houses in order to terrify them. When they saw their houses burning, they were roused to greater fury. Two of our men were killed near the houses, while we burned twenty or thirty houses. So many of them charged down upon us that they shot the captain through the right leg with a poisoned arrow.

The natives shot only at our legs, for the latter were bare; and so many were the spears and stones that they hurled at us, that we could offer no resistance. The mortars in the boats could not aid us as they were too far away. So we continued to retire for more than a good crossbow flight from the shore always fighting up to our knees in the water. The natives continued to pursue us, and picking up the same spear four or six times, hurled it at us again and again. Recognizing the captain, so many turned upon him that they knocked his helmet off his head twice, but he always stood firmly like a good knight, together with some others. Thus did we fight for more than one hour, refusing to retire farther.

An Indian hurled a bamboo spear into the captain's face, but the latter immediately killed him with his lance, which he left in the Indian's body. Then, trying to lay hand on sword, he could draw it out but halfway, because he had been wounded in the arm with a bamboo spear. When the natives saw that, they all hurled themselves upon him.

One of them wounded him on the left leg with a large cutlass, which resembles a scimitar, only being larger. That caused the captain to fall face downward, when immediately they rushed upon him with iron and bamboo spears and with their cutlasses, until they killed our mirror, our light, our comfort, and our true guide. When they wounded him, he turned back many times to see whether we were all in the boats. Thereupon, beholding him dead, we, wounded, retreated, as best we could, to the boats, which were already pulling off.

Account of the killing by Lapu-Lapu at Mactan of Fernão de Magalhães (Magellan), from Relazione del Primo Viaggio Intorno al Mondo by Antonio Pigafetta (1525), trans. James A. Robinson (1906)

lauds

These are the early morning hours, the Night Office that terminates at dawn…

Sparse Talent Squandered

I've lived longer than Thoreau but
not better. Certainly not written better,
although few of any age can
say they have. Spent not nearly
enough time in a canoe in Maine.

I've lived longer than Poe and
happier, but the horrors of the
blood spring a page just as
sure as spring days do loved
ones eager for more than my company.

I've lived longer than Fitzgerald his
boat long since surrendered to the
current while mine marooned in rushes
borne neither to the past nor
the future one paddle erect in muck.

I'm catching up to Richard Wright
and Emily Dickinson whose mirrors would
have envied mine—white and male
and free—and who made great
art despite the slings of outrageous fortune.

These words, too, lounge on an
easy couch while I do other
things with what little time I
have remaining until I end
up on the poster *Sparse Talent Squandered*.

And that's it—my big idea—
a biography series about people not
listed among the great but people
like me for whom a single life
never got started for whom the main

channel of the river diverged along
the way in all of this
tall grass when the water table
dropped a drought of a life human
a broken poetic form

Autogenes in the Fields

among rows of morning
slant sun apple saplings
I planted years ago
a strange spangle of
dewy gray and white fur
then farther down the row
a ruined tail a thin
rope of soggy tatter
after that a long tendril
of intestines in the mud
an angular
counterpoint to the windfall
yellow apples
all over the ground the
bounty that drew
the rabbit that drew the
hawk my apples
my apples
my apples

Divide

down in the valley the whole world
shakes off sleep
rumbles to industrial life
slag piles to the horizon
black warts on the skin of morning mist

down there somewhere is the
Happy Ears Popcorn Company
with Stosh at the timeclock punching
everyone in at 7:30 whether they're here or there
and here my back to this pine trunk

needles in my hair
the taste of autumn in my mouth
a rocky outcrop with a single tent
a single man on the morning ridge
like a dew drop

balanced
that will flow to the Atlantic or to the Pacific
depending on how hard the morning breeze
blows
right
now

The 6 Train and the Omega

mornings on the 59th Street uptown 6
platform boys and girls from 10 Catholic schools
vector and collide
all day it's our only shot
to attract the opposite sex
some are better at this than others
skirts and ties dance in the hot breeze and
I'm studying Kepler's laws of planetary motion
measuring the ellipses the girls make as they pass me by

the crowd parts the chatter stops
it's my friend Veneziano all eyes on him
his hair a conductive copper
blonde that teslas radiant like starstuff

he's a quasar on this platform
with gold rimmed glasses dark lenses
silk shirt open wide at the collar
he chats up some Marymount freshman
her blue plaid skirt billows up as
the number 6 Lexington Avenue local
momentums up the platform
the density of Veneziano's
hair draws her to him decays her orbit
we crowd onto the train

her eyes flash and singe in the hairspray corona
at 77th her friends tug at her elbow
she reaches escape velocity just outside of
Veneziano's event horizon
the doors close and the train rolls uptown

I say V man she would
have followed you anywhere
he checks his look in the door glass

it's like a law of nature he says
she just wants her time in the sun

the train decelerates into the light at 86th

he looks at me full on and I have to turn away

The Rumor of Love

The morning after
The wake you
Turn your face
Into the rain
The desert rain on
Fort Monmouth dunes
A formal garden
When death's the subject
Sandy Hook, her
Poison ivy legs
Mud between her toes
The rumor of love
Highlands Twin Lights
My arm around her shoulder
We walk east
She and I who miss her most

Destroyers load their nukes at Earle

Harm Lay I

~~Hail~~ Mary, full of ~~grace,~~
the Lord ~~is with you.~~
~~Blessed~~ are you ~~among women,~~
~~and~~ blessed is ~~the fruit of~~ your womb, ~~Jesus.~~
~~Holy~~ Mary, Mother of ~~God,~~
~~pray for us~~ sinners,
~~now~~ and ~~at the hour of our~~ death.

mary
      full of
      the lord
      are you
      blessed is
      your womb
mary
      mother
      of sin
      and death

Picture the congregation at 9:00 mass, the children in uncomfortable clothes thinking about bagels and the parents trying to stop the words on the page from draping towels over their heads hungover. Imagine the young mother in the children's room spat up upon husband in the back row with the four year old and that little child saying these words in this order the way people do. Words in this order Sunday in and Sunday out all the way from Baptism until *extreme unction*, and where for these young parents but decades of hell do they lead?

The Ancestor Story

Here is the chair
and here is the window
and here I sit
watching this pen glide
across this page
spilling its insides
      all known things must end
and the page fills with
ink that can't be
wrung from the page

the pen empties
the chair warms
the next page cringes ready
blank but for the faint trace
of its ancestor story
that gets covered by
the next pen the next ink
the next person who sees the chair
and thinks
it would be good to live
for a while in that chair
the warm blue green embrace
a comfortable habitat
to watch a poem ramify
as if it were born packed
for a long journey

What Will Kill Him and Soon

The meat of his fingers
crowds out the knuckles.
His rings no longer fit.
He leans into the jar of pickled
herring, twists it against his Christmas
sweater and grunts. Those little
fish living life under polar ice
skittish about what didn't end up eating them.
I wonder if anything makes a man afraid
when he knows exactly what will
kill him and soon?
He holds
the jar out to me.
Another thing
I won't miss,
he says.

Old Man, Drawn Brightly

After a night negotiating his mortality, on time for the appointment, the stiff and standing morning gentleman's hesitation is drawn brightly to the sun-dappled mirror in the young doctor's waiting room. His gaze ranges and darts about the whispering room, slides across the two-way mirror.

On time for the appointment, the stiff and standing morning gentleman's hesitation is arrested by the deep canyons he sees in the glass, in his face. His gaze ranges and darts about the whispering waiting room, slides across the two-way mirror. This looks, finally, like old age. I look, finally, like old age.

Arrested by the deep canyons he sees in the glass, in his face, the old man steps closer, adjusts his bifocals, squints at light quadruply refracted. This looks, finally, like old age. I look, finally, like old age. And what rivers lie at the bottom of those gorges? What forces have eroded this rock?

The old man steps closer, adjusts his bifocals, squints at light quadruply refracted. The mirror glass slides to the side with a small squeak. A woman in white sits unblinkingly revealed. And what rivers lie at the bottom of those gorges? What forces have eroded this rock? If everything is reflection and repetition, where is the me who is growing younger?

The mirror glass slides to the side with a small squeak. A woman in white sits unblinkingly revealed. She says the old man's name. He straightens painfully, stretching his back, his mind, his longevity. If everything is reflection and repetition, where is the me who is growing younger? He follows the woman in white through the inner door, but part of him remains.

She calls the old man's name. He straightens painfully, stretching his back, his mind, his longevity. After a night negotiating his mortality, he follows the woman in white through the inner door, but part of him remains drawn brightly to the sun-dappled mirror in the young doctor's waiting room.

RESPONSORIAL PSALM: The Comet She Hoped Was a God

Refrain: After the comet she hoped was a god hit the Yucatan

> she fled to the north
> while her new almighty pushed out
> clouds that banked and growled
> pursued her
> she panicked and ran as the cold wind

R: After the comet she hoped was a god hit the Yucatan

> the cold summer wind that blew branches
> from trees clawed at her back
> she stumbled farther on
> marveling at new pain
> the rain just begun changed to ice then snow
> she panicked and ran as the cold wind

R: after the comet she hoped was a god hit the Yucatan

> she cowered beneath the sky
> the iron sky
> like she was deep inside the ocean
> or buried alive
> she cowered beneath the sky
> she panicked and ran as the cold wind

R: After the comet she hoped was a god hit the Yucatan

Crawled She New Booming Bed

We planted seraph script and tote
      under the blooms green bed
As ancient weems crawled this and they
      she lived as happy wife
I husband true for ingénue
      was fashion for a while
Proud robin red the clothing wash
      suburban breeze would wave
The privet hedge blown cul de sac
      denuded flesh enticed
Beyond betrayal's cliff a belch
      new islands growing bold
Now late the garden mud and spring
      absorb your mercies lack
Pacific heights asteam aboil
      black stone to catch salt waves
All Eden in a day my dear
      now we two selves apart
Your chance now to exhale my dear
      you held your breath for me
As ancient weems crawl this and they
      crawled she new booming bed
I'll plant no seraph script and tote
      until these blooms brown dead

How to Pray to a Spider

in the men's room stall
on the tile floor between my toes
a tiny spider surveys her realm
her life of web weaving and
eating the toughest kid on
the block eight-eyed monster
with mandibles from here to
next week and she stops too
curious she might be at the
feeling she is being watched
from above that she is not
alone shall I give her a sign
that I am here that I built all
this for her well not exactly
I and not exactly for her but that
her safe passage across the
floor is my doing that I could
end it all with a flick of my
toe a sign like maybe waving
my arm in front of the sun letting
its shadow pass—

(while I wrote that, the spider vanished the way people do sometimes; they ebb, wane, and dismay the gods who need them)

Private Property

Where that particle board boathouse is? The water laps against that dock now as it once hissed then the knees of phragmites. The path winds around the lake as it did then, too, and my feet take me down to the ancient mill dam where the smooth river curves over the edge, becomes a living, white sheet, the gentle respiration of the lake coming to jeweled light for a moment, then collecting itself for the slow downhill run to the Atlantic.

Thorns bracket the lakeshore. Turtles show up twice a summer. Beavers splat their tails as if they'd been here all along. And the last trees are cleared as the beavers watch, for the last McMansion. The limitless forest of my childhood the deer and bears and all of it.

Goodbye to all that.

Seasons later, my kid with me and I try to explain the walk upstream through the swamp or the longer route along the ridge, to a lake of my own. She's having none of it. We're in a development like any other. But I could have told them they'd never get rid of the phragmites. My lake is under your lawn. I swam it for endless summers, right through your basement and into your pipes where I'll rattle all night until all of you hedge fund managers sink Usher-like into my past.

Meditation: Be Joyful!

There's rosemary
That's for remembrance
Pray, love, remember
And there is pansies
That's for thoughts
There's fennel for you
And columbines: there's rue
For you; and here's some for me
We may call it herb-grace o'Sundays
O you must wear your rue with
A difference. There's a daisy
I would give you some violets
But they withered all when
My father died
They say he made a good end—
And will he not come again?
No, no. He is dead.
He will never come again.

Dear maid, kind sister, sweet Ophelia, Hamlet 4.5

hora media

the midday hours, the time of shadows...

This Noncommittal Gravity

a field of yellow and
green haze of gnats cicada
buzz the red-tailed hawk

reclines on a blue bed
looks up at me like
an ancient god expecting peeled

grapes too hot to talon
dive to deign to sinew
rip she drifts instead lazy

open mouthed serene knowing and
knowing I'll fall into her
knees bent I curl my

toes rebel into the brown
remains my fingers hang against
this noncommittal gravity this patch

of earth rises toward the
hawk who rides the thermals
a purple martin skims between

us avian acolyte with a
branch to fan it is
easier still to let go

the martin chortles disembark from
that body prostrate yourself to
the sky the air sparks electric

with the afternoon thunderhead my
fingers sweep the grassy sky
reverent with *kree* of hawk

A Martyr Made When Lustful Suitors Came

below the chapel high school locker room
where teenage boys and lunch time sing alive
them and the stones unsatisfied

they've all just gone the chapel left to me
its dusty marble statues dim stained glass
candles flicker red in hope

it's twenty-five till calculus begins
the din of footsteps closing door stillness
my eyes adjust to silent pews

she's there up there where priests and deacons stent
her shoulder to the congregation stiff
her chin in profile raised aloof

teresa my teresa name of love
a martyr made when lustful suitors came
drawn by your reputation pure

I step high over the rail to see
her face again as she looks clean through time
the past and future sing with her

those men heard you yes in every soft hello
they heard you yes you fled out the back door
across those winter fields the wind

the sculptor had to make a woman true
her shoulders square and soft cheekbones persuade
her flowing hair frames gentle smile

teresa my teresa name of love
you ran to the clifftop and hid from them
like dogs on a scent the men pursued

the sculptor had to make a woman true
but he didn't need to cut her dress so low
the triangle of pink that plunged

these men said decide to die or wed
to fall from grace or from this precipice
to die preserve your honor pure

I fell like a mass falling through the sky
I heard her yes and reached my fingers out
and traced my name in the pinkish dust

the story says you leaped into blue sky
your body hit the boulder field below
while your soul already danced in heaven's light

the triangle of pink that drew me here
the closest I had come to woman's flesh
I heard you yes I swear I did I heard you yes

Made Down Here by the Breaking of Things

Villejo's novel washed up on my desk one day.
The boy, himself, drowned, the boy, himself, on the page for me,
his teacher, to assess evaluate condemn damn grade or love.
Villejo, a kid who thinks himself talented brilliant
but (bad luck) has to prove it
not just with talk but with—words.
Villejo, he's like an eager swimmer,
at the warm sunny edge of the icy void
whose dwellers below scuttle and claw.
Villejo, they watch you sideways through kelp
and swirling sand that's been eroded,
abraded by groundswell, current,
and storm, made down here by the breaking of things,
pushed up and out, mounded and duned,
jeweled briefly by sunshine.
Villejo, your words are emissaries
from the places where the names of treasures
and dead things are written in sand!

Ranger Flight Roger, Point Pleasant, New Jersey

I knew all the answers to the pilot exam,
knew about weather
and radio, wind speed
celestial navigation
knew about gliding when engine cut out
wing whistles that scream in a stall
tune-ups and airstrip patterns below
landing in water, in fields, on highways, in trees
knew about take-offs and taxis
navigation
instrumental
visual flight, night blindness.

In short, I could make a rudder dance.

Faking my way through the colorblind test
was another matter.
Walking back across the airport lot to my
ground bound Ranger, that heavy thing,
      all drag, no lift that long walk,
from the front door of the pilot school in Lakewood
to my front seat,
I know what to do.
I slip behind the wheel and drive
down route 88
aiming for the sea
in the only vehicle
on land or air I am licensed to fly.

I accelerate, ninety degree heading, boardwalk rising
the runway lies ahead like a great false dawn
I punch the gas to rotation speed,
pull back on the steering wheel
to nose up and over the boardwalk with its
> dark gray concrete pilings,
> the drab planks,
> the white lemonade stand with
> Fourth of July tanned bodies gawking at the spectacle of
> me and my Ford
as we climb up and over the beach
landing gear stowed, bank gently to the south,
I dip a wing to the wide, gray sea.

Reasons to be Cheerful, Part 4

The Lord God whispered:
you mustn't blame yourself
your mommy had a baby inside of her and then it died
or rather he died your little brother

The Lord God revealed:
he would have been a sweet beautiful boy
full of life and fun
ready to play with you

The Lord God sang:
oh come to me my dear come to me
yes I'll hold you close
these things just happen for no reason

The Lord God opined:
maybe mommy ate something bad and got a little sick
it could be anything, ice cream, candy,
or it could be stress

The Lord God remonstrated:
you know how mommy has to yell
at you to clean up your room
that's what stress is

The Lord God hissed:
there, there let's just think
pretty thoughts about your
darling little brother

The Lord God speculated:
it could have been a fall,
like when your mommy tripped
over your toys last week on the stairs

The Lord God sighed:
okay the truth
my sweet beautiful jesus
wanted him in heaven that's all

The Lord God cooed:
jesus looked down on your rooftop
and said he's too sweet for you
I'm keeping him all for myself
and he was right
by definition he was right
run along to bed
now dear yes right now

On Our Reptilian Origin

whence the snow the cold that penetrates the walls
a thin skein of ice on window panes
a second skin molting crystalline and pure
I don't remember seeing the snow start
        here inside the warming sun shines
        through porch windows into my study
        where I sit and push a pen across this page
        as if it were a snake tensed striking
        again and again at a skittish small thing
        just past the next pen stroke
        out of fangs' reach
        that leaves a jagged black line across the page
        where they have missed their prey
outside a new white skin smooths
over vertebral complications
that freeze as if beneath layered gauze
as sharp memory lies bandaged beneath webbed experience
        my hand stiffens its reptilian self who dreams
        of basking in sun-dappled summer lowlands
        instead testifies to deepening cold
        the skin of decay

Any Precious, Fragile Thing

the pen on the page reveals a river of ink
that runs downhill and finds its channel.

if only I could hold this pen the right way
hold it like a lost lover a newborn child

a dying parent, any precious, fragile thing
if I could only hold it the right way

it would find in the page between these
black lines the faint impression of

words already formed footprints in the
low tide silt filled with oily water

where we have already walked
that flash rainbows onto our backs

when sunlight hits the lower Passaic River
just right

Watergate

Louie was so proud of that flood
in '72, an election year, when
the roiling mud of the
Susquehanna, that uninspiring river,
busted through the levee
at Forty-Fort and bulldozed
the valley, uprooted trees, cars, and
corpses (the cemetery at the river
bend shady and cool) all the way
down Wyoming Avenue to Kingston,
Plymouth, and south.

A muddy ocean, ten feet deep
that drew a sharp brown line
exactly that high inside and
outside of everything. Louie
opened his desk drawer for me, six
feet below the high-mud mark, and
pulled out a picture of the young him
and President Nixon, who
dropped in by helicopter
looking as surprised as anyone to find
himself submerged in America.

You Ever Music Me

sing to these roses if you will
        they mean nothing to me
no harbinger of pleasant sun
        no lilt aroma sweet
no tide or hue your boardwalk planks
        no petals o'er your ear
no rootlets through the clear sea glass
        or beachside showers nude
they mean nothing to me

sing to these roses if you stoop
        they stand for just themselves
I bought them earlier today
        an optimistic haze
in truth I hoped that we could sing
        love's tender harmony
stems my lyrics red the beat
        rhythm your melody
you ever music me

sing to these roses charity
        these roses might be me
their soft edge tough against sea breeze
        inside the plastic sheet
imagined notes of mad desire
        you're on to something new
you hear skee ball and hot dog bar
        coin mouth of claw machines
I just can't music you

sing to these roses they are me
        the ocean waves and sun
red harbingers of sunset walks
        love's lilt aroma sweet
high tide moonrise on shimmer path
        green stems tucked by your ear
brave rootlets through the clear sea glass
        raw beachside shower nude
we're music you and me
we're music you and me

Meditation: Healing of the Water

19 The people of Jericho said to Elisha, *Look, lord, this town is a pretty good town. You can see that for yourself. The thing is, our water's messed up we can't grow nothing.*

20 *Bring me a new bowl, something real nice,* Elisha said. *And put salt in it.* They did what he asked, even though they had no idea what the old coot was up to.

21 Then Elisha went out to the town's spring, waved his arms around, and threw the salt into the spring, saying, *The Lord just spoke to me! 'I have healed this water!* the Lord said. *Won't cause you no trouble no more never and nohow."*

22 And the water has remained pure to this day, exactly as Elisha said it would.

23 Even though they wanted him to stay to install a mountain or two for the tourists, Elisha decided to take a trip to Bethel. As he was walking along the road, some children from Jericho followed him and made fun of him. *Get out of here, baldy!* they said. *Keep right on walking, baldylocks!*

24 He turned around, got real mad, and called down a curse in the name of the Lord. Two bears came out of the woods and tore forty-two of the boys to pieces their own mamas wouldn't recognize.

25 Elisha continued on to Bethel and then Mount Carmel, spreading the Lord's message, before returning to Samaria.

The Second Book of Kings, Chapter 2, Verses 19-24

vespers

sunset: you get so very few of these…

Breakwater Serenade

Serenade me!
she screamed into the wind
her sweet, unfaithful self
and the storm supplicated at her feet
in waves that
shattered into mist
along the breakwater

She, wet, with bones soaked in brine
She, her sweet, unfaithful self, with mottled skin
She, wet, of salted consciousness
She, her sweet, unfaithful self,
for whom nothing could be denied

She demanded a daily storm
and the green and white tumult
brought his gift to her,
power life transience memory
taught her to dissipate
into mist against his breakwater

She, wet, with bones soaked in brine
She, her sweet, unfaithful self, with mottled skin
She, wet, of salted consciousness
She, her sweet, unfaithful self,

for whom nothing could be denied
She, her sweet, unfaithful self,
for whom nothing could be denied

Serenade me!
she screamed into the wind

We Live Here

they live there
they live right there
it's their summer home that
pair of sandhill cranes in the
swampy lee between the zamboni-
dumped ice pile and the CN tracks they
live there thin heads rise above their reedy
world the ancestral memory of vast and empty
North America before house cats on Vegas benders
and highway noise and this cargo shorts hockey dad
standing with his hands on hips staring down at them
they raise the old alarm to defend within reason their home
and know wings are to make an escape when logic fails
the harsh melody of
their alien trills makes
this nesting pair Ghidorah
in my mind and
me that hockey dad
suddenly back in time
in my after-school
clothes crosslegged supporting mac
and cheese with hot
dogs chopped into it
(my mom's best recipe)
the 4:30 movie on
Channel 7 Destroy All
Monsters! the best day
all Monster Week long

I know why those sandhill cranes bray the ancient alarm to
defend within reason their home they're smarter than I am
to recognize what is important what is vital and defend it
like it matters with both logic and a full heart their
words theremin the cattails you don't belong here
biped brother although you seem to belong
everywhere else but might we please have
this strip of swamp for ourselves at
least for this brief northern summer
season to teach language to these
newly-shelled whelps?
we live here we
live right here

The River in the Rain

she finds a quiet corner
in the picnic shelter
talks on the phone
she forgets me
I'm sure
when she walks
away like that
and her voice becomes
the whispered reply to
the river patience

and I and this flatware
share the blue and white
tablecloth with
empty glasses
the crackers and cheese
saturated with better weather hopes

the soft hiss of the river in the rain
the wine and the glass
the cheese to the cracker
the sound of her voice without mine
all is balance

Moreno's Son

Out the door of Morristown General
the sun squints in the west,
Moreno revs his two-seater
glides out onto New Jersey blacktop.

Route 57 ribbons north through
Morris Plains and Parsippany where
traffic swells
like pregnancy
but the late afternoon highway's curves are
straightened at Mount Tabor by the
Boonton Line's tracks.

Then 57 dies a little bit, contracted under
ten lanes of Route 80, like the Interstate
had an child in its belly and
miscarried.

Down the hill is a low long row of apartments
where Moreno's empty sack
blows along a muddy embankment
above the Rockaway River
a vulture sleeps in a leafless tree.

Jeremy, the Boot Camp God

Your room is not what I expected: I thought
Of dirty clothes, of dirty magazines
13 years of too much to handle—

The priests know what to do with
Boys like you.

Bed made, blank walls, drawers empty, musty and hot.
Did you live here at all?
October came—no word from you.
Report card: abstract, thin.

I am in your bed now, in your made bed,
The ceiling cracks intersect
Loose plaster falls
Water stains.

Even before I can see that the window is painted shut,
Even before I see the crucifix on the wall above the sink,
The word "escape" flashes into my mind.
Where have you gone, Jeremy?
Where the hell have you gone?

Ironbound

Purple harbors of blood through tissue-paper skin
Brown spots like muddy puddles over the bones of the Earth

She scrubs with those hands the black spots on the fry pan
A siren in the street, the people upstairs dance.

The tide rushes in, covers the mud flats in Ironbound.

Her daughter, Susan, teaches in Miami, writes poetry in
A big house on the beach, she's married to her second banker.
Michael's a rabbi in Westport, leads tours to Israel
Every winter, mails magazines to his mom.
The youngest, Rachel, never came back from Marseilles.

Twice a day, every day, a salt wind strokes the lace curtain
    above the sink
She stops, unfolds her creased fingers, breathes deep.
She touches the damp edge of the fabric, the embroidered
    texture,
Steam rises from the dishes, the wet air pushes in.

The tide, the salt air, covers the flatlands of Ironbound,
Her home. And she plunges elbow deep
into the hot water, closes her eyes, and smiles.

Dragons in Subway Tunnels

(spoken) Teenage Fanclub at CBGB's and some girl
Tony thinks I might like.
Tonight's the night, he promises,
that you and I will begin.

(sung) And from tar roof tops people
lean and watch
in the soft summer afternoon heat.
Below them I crusade
in the flush of innocence
through the holy land of NYC.
St. Mark's Place across town,
I am a warrior bound
to take back CBGB's from the
unbelievers I am a warrior bound.

(spoken) There's Mojo's Bar
the scene five years later of our
last fight ever when I bought
you a cactus for your birthday and
it only got worse from there

(sung) A grate in the street cuts loose a roar
a blast from the Bleecker Street 6
boils off my sweat a dragon's white eyes
the future comes on like that
down dark tunnels below city streets

beyond all human sight
tonight's the night that Tony promises
you and I will begin

(spoken) Teenage Fanclub at CBGB's
and some girl he thinks I might like

(sung) So from tar roof tops people
lean and watch
in the soft summer afternoon heat.
Below them I crusade
in the flush of innocence
through the holy land of NYC.
St. Mark's Place across town,
I am a warrior bound
to take back CBGB's from the
unbelievers I am a warrior bound.

(spoken) Teenage Fanclub at CBGB's and some girl
Tony thinks I might like.
Tonight's the night, he promises,
that you and I
you and I will begin.

Her Squid Uncooked

I could have walked faster than the bus
bounced along the stone alleys of Athens
through lifetimes of neighborhoods, the people
doing their thing, living life.
Athens, Tokyo, New York—it doesn't matter,
house upon house, more shops and bars.

The woman across the aisle
sags under groceries, smiles at me vaguely,
as if she were carved from marble.
It's her end-of-day smile,
not an offer to teach me
to say ευχαριστώ   [thank you]
Hand on the seat in front of her,
she shifts her weight forward, shouts,
Stasis! and the bus knows
Greek better than I do.
It slows, stops.
People get off.
She gets off.

I press my cheek to the dusty window
to watch her walk down the dark side street.
where she remains
her Feta whole

her squid uncooked
the workday over as
the night spreads down from the Acropolis
the coming of the night in Athens
a garden of white statues in deep shadow

A Theory of the Afterlife

listen carefully because I will say this only once
listen carefully because I will only say this once

From the moment of birth
your many ghosts
brighten your eyes
sparkle the world
dance and sing
play and explore
       but ghosts impatient
       catch rides across the
       green earth vanish like
       sky color as night rises
and older now
a life well-lived
a single piece
your ghosts dispersed
and your final light
rests reluctant and pale
enough to dent a pillow
but no more
when at last it finds the courage to
leave your body
to see if there is anything next
you wish this ghost well as you
have godsped the others
you remain inanimate

yet wise to the murmur of the
unfamiliar the others those strange
many who have touched you
the ghosts of
everyone you've ever loved
that after you've gone
explode into the world
the memory of it all

only I will say this
listen carefully

The Bad Knish

I read that OJ Simpson likes Rueben
sandwiches at Katz's Deli that night
when we first met and they served up the only
truly god-awful knish I have ever tasted but
the yellow mustard saved it for a couple of bites
and we laughed while I globbed yellow on like
the big dispensers at the Meadowlands
where the mustard is sometimes
                              tampered with
by the boys before the games so I go for
the little packets like the ketchup ones
you used to explode on the Houston St. sidewalk
under your heel spreading red all
over the ground like a zombie had been cut in
half or like a murder out of jealous impotent rage
that you'd feel too if you saw your
love (not me) with another
crossing against the light just outside
Katz's on the way to the Angelika anger that
we've all felt but never acted on most of us
just chewed that Rueben a little harder ingesting
the strength to go on without you

All of the Optimistic Religions

poetry readings work best when snarky
ever notice that? how rare the risks and
how common the crappy punchlines
I've chuckled the polite titter when
someone makes a funny
I can do funny all day
I can make anybody laugh just ask
my wife who has seen me naked
but these shallow gurgles in poetry skirts
my scaly butt's more poetry than
you rhyming cancer with morris dancer
you laugh a less real part of me than
watching a wobbler score her first real goal
or hearing for the millionth time
Born to Run and seeing this time
a new way a boy can look so hard
a way I just found in my fiftieth year
this boy watching those girls who comb their
hair in rear view mirrors and seeing myself
in them in the genes of my daughter
whom I drop off for work and she gives herself a
quick look in my mirror and steps out the door
see you later she chirps and passes the
dumpster on the way to the back door
of the restaurant and leaves me with an empty minivan
and a mirror akimbo no looking back
nosed into the curb and someday my girl we'll get to that place

we really want to go and we'll walk in the sun
but till then we need to keep hoping that one
of these poetry readings—just one without a poet named
Komunyakaa or Plath—will turn out to be
something other that this transparent crapfest
of nothing ever the nothing that presses you into your seat
chokes the breath out of you and hisses *this
is what it's like to be dead and forgotten* when all of the
optimistic religions got it way wrong about
the afterlife and this is how it feels after
you had the infinite expanse of white paper
in front of you and a perfectly good pen
and you decided to write that steaming pile of crap
that you felt had to be read today to all of us
you arrived here today like a million years
of erosion to my sandstone hopes for transcendence
my teeth like stalagmites clenched
hoping you die before you fin—

Meditation: What Do All the People Know?

Gods possessing an agricultural significance are nearly always war-gods, but that is because they bring the fertilizing thunder clouds, and therefore possess the lightning arrow or spear. But Ishtar is specifically a goddess of the class of Persephone or Isis, and her identification with battle must be regarded as purely accidental. In later times, in Assyria, she was conceived as the consort of Asshur, head of the Assyrian pantheon, in days when a god or goddess who did not breathe war was of little use to people like the Assyrians, who were constantly employed in hostilities, and this circumstance naturally heightened her reputation as a warlike divinity. But it is at present her original character with which we are occupied, indeed in some texts we find that, so far from being able to protect herself, Ishtar and her property are made the prey of the savage En-lil, the storm-god:

The unconsecrated foe entered my courts,
placed his unwashed hands upon me,
and caused me to tremble.
Putting forth his hand
He smote me with fear.
He tore away my robe
and clothed his wife therein;
he stripped off my jewels
and placed them upon his daughter.
Like a quivering dove upon a beam
I sat.

Like a fleeing bird from my cranny
swiftly I passed
from my temple.
Like a bird
they caused me to fly.

Such is the plaint of Ishtar, who in this case appears to be quite helpless before the enemy.

-*Myths and Legends of Babylonia and Assyria* by Lewis Spence (1917)

compline

*When then all are
in their places, let
Compline be said; and
after coming out from
Compline let no one
be at liberty to
talk to anyone again.*

-Rule of Benedict XLII

Love Stings Drone and Lonely

it wasn't the drunk and desperate
crowd whose ears will ring with dull and gloried
memory of this blues jam near closing
it wasn't the VFW hall decked for
Valentino's no it was
her gray eyes two eyes
those gray eyes like she
wasn't fully made like
a dream a minute after
waking two gray bells
that sustained forever
that's all I saw beyond

my sax's bell, those two eyes
and I didn't see her move in close
until her hand slicked up the cuff
of my jeans fingered raw skin
sparks blasting out through
the stops in the horn like
she was playing me
the three of us screaming
into the night
raising everything we could
the roof beam beer lights
carnival sounds dancing crowd

the throaty growl of a 12 bar blues
tenor sax in heat the roiling majesty
of any tight bar band on any tight
Saturday night volume blasting away
doubt in waves of pure sound
when you're riding on the root
the train is in the station her bags are packed
then you rise to the fourth
that same train rolling down the tracks
then you climb to the fifth
you know she ain't never coming back
so when the fifth dropped back down to the root

our solo ended and she slipped away
like sound waves in the night
her gray eyes turned to
mist in the rattle and hum
the bright stage lights
a dream a minute after waking
a train's distant rumble, long gone
I left my sax in the stand and ran to the parking lot
watched every car that left until I stood
alone in the early morning ice gravel
a night bird's good night solo stings
drone and lonely in my ringing ears

I Never Beat Her at Scrabble, Not Once

I mean, where were you
when we all learned tact?
It's not you, it's me
I'm not ready—you're too
good for me—any of the above
but not you, in your red
dress cut low, leaning
across the table, full moons
eclipsing the gloss black table top
the band played
I Wanna Be Sedated and
you said the word
like a command
like a prayer
like you dropped it on
a triple word after I gave you
the corner and a chance to
cut me a break for once
and let me play squeeze
instead, you gave me extinct
and sealed another game

Achingly Paisley-Less

a rumor of swirling paisley
scarves and street corner meetings
a museum where her image is preserved under glass

the story of her
broods behind black iron gates
and stone battlements with
windows that mumble grayly
        in half-forgotten dreams
          that fill my notebooks like ciphers

a facade of parapets and gargoyles inerasable
stone faces above that heavy oak door
cherubim by another name with their flaming
swords the Latin inscription mocks
it is better to have loved…

not even the walk to the door bearing
        the weight of my forgetfulness
not even the scrilled oak door itself
        the edenic image of green trees in
        deep shadow
not even the hall past that heavy heavy door
not even the dim marble lobby with
        the dinosaur bones of youthful
        trust—not even these but

just these black gates outside have stopped me
my cold fingers twine the iron now
the gloom drains my paltry heat now

the museum of your memory
looms silently behind
these black gates that
seem to whisper you might have
                            you could have
                            you should have

all of love's wonders inside and
outside here the cold gray sky the rising wind
the present moment and all
future days and weeks without her

I am tear-eyed and blind
achingly paisley-less

Stafford's Deer
on reading "Traveling Through the Night"

The dead pregnant deer in Stafford's poem got rolled
down the pebbly embankment and splashed into the river.
But if he had cared at all, he would have
bludgeoned that belly just to make sure the
warm life inside never knew anything but the
beauty of the womb, the mystery of momentum.

Sometimes we
think we are strong
enough to kick
ourselves
over embankments
trying to reach those
baptisms we think
we deserve. Sometimes
we think we are strong
enough to handle
the invitations that come our
way like bright lights in
the night that dazzle our eyes
apprehend us, and break our bones.
Times like that, we don't need a poet
telling us which way is down.
It's all down from there.

Strawberry Jam Apocalypse

I thought we'd both die
(the irony!)
once we got laughing so hard.
A battle (to the death!) of wits
at that last supper:
I grew up on a farmageddon
wanted to be a schoolmarmageddon.
Please pass the chicken parmageddon.
A doctor's promise: first, do no harmageddon
My favorite book: The Bell Jarmageddon
Ouch! My neckageddon,
my legageddon, my armageddon.
Which armageddon?
Disarmageddon.

Before dessert (toast and strawberry jam)
she cleaned the dishes.
I couldn't talk her out of it,
in fact, she made me take out the trash, too,
on the earth's final night.
I stowed it carefully against the rising wind
the night sky awash in streaks of color
the asteroid breaking up in all that beauty.

A spider in the porch light wove her web,
the crickets whispered "sex!"
I spent these last years chasing her.

Tonight, the chase ends, one way or another.
A hand on my shoulder
my love—ah!
She's let me catch her at last!

And I breathe, *kiss me kiss me*
with your strawberry jam apocalypse!

The Sound of Rain in a Bucket

sad memory
is the sound of rain in a bucket
beneath a leaky gutter in the night
by a window closed against darkness and the
wet
        wet
                bell
                        bell
a single staccato note, like a pulse
the night makes audible by accident.

memory is patient
as humble as the heart
as accidental as a discarded
metal bucket that amplifies the rain.

later,
my lover's heartbeat, long-stilled
audible in my dream,
my ear
against her bare chest
somehow whole again
against her bare chest
somehow whole again.
in the dream that face, her face
is living living living

I've heard in distant thunder
seen in steaming earth in broken clouds in rain
seen her at the end of my hand

but, ah, her face!
the image fades
as it did once before.
too soon!
the clouds part, make way for the dawn.
and I wake, bitter,
to a sparkling springtime Sunday!

Not Pure Enough to Burn

Me and Empty on a
slagheap at midnight
drinking apple wine
from dirty bottles
we're weak
coal, not pure enough
to burn, but the weight
of slag heats the mountain
past combustion and
we float above this black
hill riding an updraft

the heat ripples the
city lights the black
rim of the valley
the circumference of what
is possible and what is not

we drift home ride
the low rumble of the
crematorium whose ashes
settle on our city like prophecy

The Secret Of Electricity

12:34 am: The Witness

you walked alone through my secret place
and I saw you do it
from a passing car
I thought only I knew
that after dark on softest nights in early fall
      beneath tall cream white electric lamps
audible fragrant circles of light are cast in thick grass;
        and in these circles of light insects gather,
          mass, climb, chirp, clutch, dig, grab:
           a movable carpet of devotion
did you find communion with
this simple brightness that translucent wings find effortlessly?

1:09 am: The Investigation

I ran back and looked for you, did you know that?
Made an excuse, ran back and looked for you
my tall, cream white crush

dew-stuck skirt to slight thighs
playing with that rose quartz necklace

that turns light into
needles .

you were here less than an hour ago-
where did you go?

I should have been there
to show the bright circles to you
the teeming pilgrims
and stay out all night
wait for a freight train to roll through
count the cars
a confession:
I was lured by her bright light
you should have seen her smile at me
I, a luna moth pulled,
without centrifuge, toward her warm electric brightness

Who told you to come here, to this place, without me?
Where my life's secrets play like hunger?

2:29 am: The Rationalization

I lie awake and remember my NYFD friend who once told me that fire fighters first touch dubious wires with the backs of their hands. His lesson: live current in the palm closes hands tight, burns from the inside out.

3:24 am: The Burning

I never found you
a quiet resignation and back home again
to shuffle and deal a single hand of lonely man's solitaire,
but I've got to know:
Am I grounded?
Am I safe from lightning?

And when I dream tonight
will I find that electric circle in the grass, again, as it has been
    for 20-odd years,
And find myself
elated?
me, a climber, chirper, clutcher, digger, grabber?
casting blindly for the secret of electricity, the cause of the light?

And what about these burns I see on this right hand,
covering this stomach,
staining these sheets?

The Biologist and His Daughter

Gallup polls say nearly all his demographic peers have bought
one middle age college bred white men bankers lawyers all
buy into now communication palm but he does nothing of the
    sort no

likes his meetings face to frontward likes his letters stamped
    and sealed by
hands and tongues and penmanship for all the wonders
    instant mailing
all the facetime worldly skyping heat the pockets of these
    magnates

richer than the world imagined knowledge flicked impatient
    fingers
now the poorest high school kid has information at her
    beckon
libraries encyclopedias monthly moods and new band
    soundings

everything the world has gathered calls to her 24/7
daughter floats with disconnect he longs to reach her make
    her laugh the
way she did when she was small the world it seems to him
    escapes her

what about the wide green Earth to share with me he wonders
    does she
miss the subtler calls of insects waves of color midnight sky

the names of things observed and entered memorized
    ancestral truths and

simple observation skills and looking closely art and faces
peering under bridges brightly seeing all the life below us
underneath the stones and sky the dirt beneath his fingers
    tells of

days alone atop the ridgeline magnifying lichen microbe
peering at the life exploding wonders all the way unfolding
stars and sun and moon and comet visit his imagination

talks with David Attenborough notes it all in diary friends
Carl Sagan and Richard Feynman vivid dreams connected lively
Isaac Newton E.O. Wilson low tech storage ink and paper

Rachel Carson Richard Dawkins faithful friends for all of life
    these
home again she reads his journal meant for walking reading
    endless
meant to share with daughter lovely he hopes she finds truth
    and humor

she politely clears her throat and stoops to kiss his forehead
    dainty
dear poor dad mosquito bitten needs a shower needs a
    haircut
here's lasagna yes I know how cooking apps are free to
    download

see you later going out to see a movie with my friends and
be back later on this evening she was right delicious pasta
she was right he was surprised that she could make this make
   it for him

self contained she is and secure walks alone with friends in
   pocket
worries more about him than he knows or wants to understand
what was it that he objected all his peers connected mobile

he alone stays solitary no connected to the wrong world
filling time with aspiration libraries and books antique what
good is it to know the wide world know the names of worms
   and spiders

understand celestial bodies grasp the nuance subatomic
she was right the bathtub felt good miracle hot water flows
   from
walls of first world habitation now and maybe decades
   henceforth

bathtub solitary Sunday yes that's it the solitary
all his peers could facetime bath time laughing now the old
   man thinks that
all of civilized creation leads wrinkled men who soaked and
   steamed

for daughters fretting marinara bathtub solitary Sunday
generations who migrate to very different habitats he
dreams he is a bug pinned wriggling studied splayed and
   categorized

what good is it to clasp ones hands French kiss each cheek
    Japan they bow
time's geography calls him a loner for withdrawing social
bathtub solitary Sunday generations who migrate to

very different habitats he dreams he is a bug pinned
    wriggling
studied splayed and categorized most of life is like this he
    cogens
mostly life's like this he dreams

Bill Gillard is an award-winning teacher of creative writing and literature at the University of Wisconsin Oshkosh. His writing has appeared in dozens of journals, and he is the author of two chapbooks: *Ode to Sandra Hook and Desire, the River* and the co-author of *Speculative Modernism,* a study of the literary origins of science fiction, fantasy, and horror. He is the Fiction Editor at the literary magazine, *Masque and Spectacle,* and earned an M.F.A. from Fairleigh Dickinson University. He lives in Appleton, Wisconsin, with his wife and two daughters and is a recovering youth hockey coach.

www.ingramcontent.com/pod-product-compliance
Lightning Source LLC
Chambersburg PA
CBHW022008120526
44592CB00034B/728